D0278058

SANCTUARY
street prayers by Albert Bogle

© Sanctus Media Ltd 2012

Published by Astwood Publishing
Website: www.astwood.org.uk

ISBN 978-0-9566732-5-1

Created, Designed and Typeset by:
Sanctus Media Ltd
Grahamsdyke Avenue
Bo'ness
EH51 9DT

Tel: 01506 827217
Website: www.sanctusmedia.com
Email: office@sanctusmedia.com

Printed by:
Kelso Graphics LLP
The Knowes
Kelso
Scottish Borders
TD5 7BH

Tel: 01573 223214
Website: www.kelsographics.co.uk

Images and Photography:
www.shutterstock.com
www.istockphoto.com
Marcus Ford
Rae Manger

With thanks to Douglas Galbraith

Contents

Foreword

I am always surprised by how God reaches out to people in different ways, but He does, and He calls us to a deep abiding trust. He meets us where we are – especially on the ground of our defeat and failure. He invites us to His warm embrace and to be filled with His love. We have a faithful God and a loving God to whom all can come and seek peace.

I would like to commend this book of prayers and meditations written by the Right Rev Albert Bogle, Moderator of the General Assembly of 2012. I pray for the ministry that Albert and Martha will have in this year of office. I pray for the meetings and conversations that lie ahead and trust that God will reveal Himself in new and exciting ways.

The Most Revd and Rt Hon Dr John Sentamu,
Archbishop of York

Preface

This book has been brought together to encourage a wider audience to recognise that prayer need not be limited to highly technically theological language. Indeed prayer in its most effective form is the instantaneous cry of the heart. I have often thought when someone utters the words "My God" unthinkingly, there may be an element of disrespect to the Almighty, but could there also be an acknowledgement that in our most vulnerable moments of despair and fear we find ourselves instantly crying out to God in prayer?

Many of the prayers and meditations in this book were written to be used on the Sanctuary First website. This website seeks to connect with people of faith and no faith who wish to explore ideas about God and Christianity while surfing the net.
(www.sanctuaryfirst.org.uk).

I often refer to these prayers as 'street prayers' simply because they are not pieces of polished prose, but instantaneous thoughts that have come to mind while reflecting about passages I've been reading in the Bible or thoughts and prayers that have come to me while sitting on a plane or a train. I guess they are the thoughts of a traveller connecting with the world around.

Right Rev Albert Bogle BD MTh
Moderator of the General Assembly of the Church of Scotland 2012

SANCTUARY

Here is sanctuary.
Gulls are singing praise to God.
Stone and wood
touch earth and sky with grace.
The river laps the sand with ease.
Ancient sounds of monks
are heard in the breeze
singing songs and chants of praise –
'Holy, Holy is the Lord!'

Colm's island speaks of God:
hermit prayers can still be heard,
saints' and sinners' voices cry
amidst the ruins of our time.
Forgive our sins, redeem our lives;
we cry for sanctuary.

Prayer never ceases; it cannot die;
it descends as peace to guard the soul;
it fills the air around this ancient holy island,
and holy men still prevail.
Prayer lives on to be fulfilled;
Colm's voice still calls on God
to calm the tumult of the soul.

Look around this holy place;
remove the guns and signs of war;
restore this to a place of prayer
where troubled souls retreat
without fear
to be at one with God.

AN AMAZING WORLD

Oh God,
this is an amazing world,
yet for some
it is merciless and meaningless.
To me it's vibrant, volatile, emerging,
and I'm part of this creativity.
It's utterly amazing:
my ideas,
my memory,
my feelings,
my awareness,
my capacity to love,
my ability to respond to another;
this feeling of compassion,
the tears in my eyes,
my sense of sheer delight.
I could never recover this moment
in a million years;
it can never be found again –
yet I lived through it,
experienced it,
an ephemeral encounter with joy,
eternity touching time,
giving meaning and substance to faith,
the breath of God
cherished by my memory to nurture the future,
a promise of beauty.
Such a mystery –
a rainbow of hope
in the midst of my doubting.
Oh God,
this is an amazing world you have created,
and I'm still in it!

MYSTERY OF GOD IN CREATION

Oh God,
before I start my daily tasks
I want to say thank you
for sustaining me through the night
and for the gift of this new day.
I pray that I may be of use
in the world in which I work.
I pray that this may be a day of growth
for me and for others.
Help me to face this day
with a quiet confidence.
When challenges come,
help me to be productive and positive.
Put a break on my tongue
when I'm tempted to gossip;
give me a creative eye
to see a new perspective
when those around are ready to give up.
Give me ears to hear what is not being said
in order that the truth can prevail.

Walk with me today into your world
and I will walk with you into mine.
Your presence
will cast out all my fears
and restore a sense of peace and belonging.
Let your kingdom come and change
my heart,
my will,
my world.
Before I start my daily tasks,
I'd like to thank you
for sustaining me through last night.

I NEED TO SPEAK YOUR NAME

Creator God,
here am I,
a created being,
thinking,
feeling,
praying to you,
the Almighty.
It's just something within me I can't control.
I'm pushing on an ever opening door;
the door itself is the revelation;
it tells me your presence
is all around
in blues, greens, reds and yellows.
I need to speak your name.
I need to reach out and touch
the mystery of the one who made me.
Oh God, how majestic you are;
you take my breath away;
such beauty –
and you made me
so I could appreciate
all this wonder-filled creativity.
How absolutely amazing.
And I know there is more
I can't see.
If I could see your entire creation,
I'd die of wonder shock!
So here I am, a created being,
speaking to you, the Creator,
through an open door
in the shape of a word.
It's just another one of your mysteries.
Oh Lord,
deal with this soul patiently
for I may well forget my place
as I gently tread
in and out of your creation.

A PERFECT DAY

Lord, today was glorious,
and I just loved the view.
The soft sunlight has
given us all a rich warm glow.
Your world is quite spectacular,
the colour scheme is breath-taking.
When the sun shines,
it seems to bring out the best in everyone.
People actually talk to each other,
the TV gets turned off,
and people go for walks.

Lord, I just love this view looking over our town.
It calls from within me a prayer
I heard from a friend recently,
so simple yet so profound.
"Come down and come in".
So, Lord, I pray,
come down and come into our town,
our homes,
our shops,
our schools,
our churches;
and, above all,
come down
and come into
our hearts.

Lord,
could we be like the tree
that has been planted by the river,
flowing through our community,
bringing health and healing
to our families?
Lord, come down,
come in;
Your Kingdom come!

GOD THE BUILDER

Dear Builder God,
I've been reading about
being a living stone,
a connecting stone, a gospel stone,
one that is built in but never seen –
a building block of your kingdom.
It's got me thinking about your quarry;
you're the mason who selects the stone;
you see its shape even before it's cut;
then you cut the stone.
I'm praying that I'll hold together
during the times of your shaping.
Wield your chisel with a gentle touch;
cut away the surplus stone in my life;
make me into a useful building block;
for it is your skill that will make me live;
it is your skill that will make me of value.
You shape the stone to fit the structure.
You know the size and shape;
then you cut the next stone to fit.
Help me see that if I suffer in the shaping
it is a price worth paying
to be a useful building block
in your kingdom.
Lord, make me a gospel-shaped stone.

Lord,
you have placed us as stones together,
all in relation to you and each other,
above and below,
leaning and holding.
Make us into a holy space,
a sacred shape,
a connecting place
where others can come
and encounter your grace.

DESIGNER GOD

Lord,
I visited the Museum of Modern Art yesterday,
in New York.
Now there's a place,
to make you feel small!
Buildings towering over you.
Anyway,
I was amazed at the things I saw.
All man-made!
There was a Vincent,
all black and shiny.
No wonder Mollie took a ride on it.
We humans have an amazing eye for design.
We just love
making things,
making things work,
making things look good,
making things to please,
making things to use,
making things just to be!
Making "R Us";
it's what we do!
It got me thinking –
from where did we inherit our creativity?
You, of course!
You made an intelligent design and designers
when you made humankind.
Lord,
help me create something good today,
something that will reflect
your influence
and purpose,
something shiny
like a "Vincent"
or even a "Van Gogh".

CAN I STAY IN THE GARDEN?

Lord,
I want to be a stone that can move
but I don't want to be always rolling.
I don't want to be immovable,
I just want to be known
as the stone the Spirit moved.
I want to be seen as a living stone –
no longer a blocker
but a witness to a resurrection.
Roll me away from the grave,
but keep me always
in the resurrection garden
so that I can encounter
doubt and healing,
tears and laughter,
despair and hope,
and above all that I can perhaps
meet angels and disciples
talking with the Gardener.

STONE ROLLING GOD

Stone rolling God,
you surprise us all again.
Each act of grace surpasses the last.
You roll a stone
and reveal a mystery;
you roll a stone and the dead come to life;
you roll a stone and angels speak to humans.
You are such a generous God.
Your acts of grace are inspirational,
your talk of forgiveness is breath-taking,
your acts of forgiveness are life-changing,
your love stretches beyond
the boundaries of reason.
You are a most unreasonable God!
You turn logic on its head,
you celebrate the weak,
you inspire the elderly,
you revive the young;
you roll a stone
and the world is changed for eternity –
all in the roll of a stone!
What a roll!
What a stone!
What a God!

I FELT SHUT OUT

Lord,
I was upset;
I felt shut out.
Maybe I shut myself out!

I was the only one missing;
everyone else was there.
They were all full of it –
you know, over-excited.
It did sound exaggerated;
it was the talk of the town.

I really didn't want to hear it.
I found it very hurtful,
almost insensitive;
it all sounded too good to be true.
So I hit out.
I told them I was different,
wired in a different way.
I was rational, a reasonable man,
not easily moved or excited.

It all came out, tumbling out,
my fears,
my pre-conditions.
I told them
I need to see,
I need to feel,
I need to examine the facts.

Then you appeared.
I wasn't expecting you.
You were different –
but no different.
I saw it all with my own eyes.
Unashamedly I worshipped you;
my Lord, my God;
I'm sorry
I struggle with doubt.

LORD, WE'RE SO UNRELIABLE

Lord,
isn't it strange
we humans can be
doubters one minute
and believers the next?
At the heart of all this doubting
is a fear we might be wrong,
we might be seen to have lived a lie.

Lord,
we must seem very unreliable friends!
We agree with you one minute;
we even make promises;
but we can change very quickly;
we're such a fickle bunch.
Yet you don't give up on us;
you never seem to stop believing in us;
you make me feel ashamed;
you must have such courage to love,
to forgive,
to look vulnerable,
to embrace our doubt and still call us friends.

Lord,
I can't talk for the others
but I can talk for myself.
Help me to keep believing;
keep me faithful in all I say and do.
Forgive me when I cause others to doubt;
forgive me when I have hurt you
by my attitude,
by my actions,
by my lack of trust.
Today, standing in the light,
I address you as Lord,
and even in my darkest moments of doubt
I still need to know you are my friend.

MEET THE BEGINNERS

Lord,
I saw you were busy with some beginners last night.
I think you were talking to them about basic stuff.
You know,
basic discipleship.
They looked like children.
I joined the group for a little while.
I was standing on the edge of the circle.
I didn't expect you to notice me.
I listened in for a short time.

Lord,
if you don't mind, I'll move on ahead,
start journeying with some of the more advanced disciples.
We know where you're heading.
It's great to be in the vanguard;
we can begin to be more Spirit-led,
move more with the flow,
explore faith issues that create a challenge.
It's great to feel the freedom of the Spirit,
be less restricted.
It allows movement at a different pace.
There is absolutely no point in going over things
that you know already.
I'm sure you'll agree,
moving at the pace of the slowest is so debilitating.

What was that you said, Lord?
They are your advanced disciples!
But I didn't see anyone I knew!
No familiar faces.
In fact they were all children!
What was that –
'Of such are the Kingdom'?

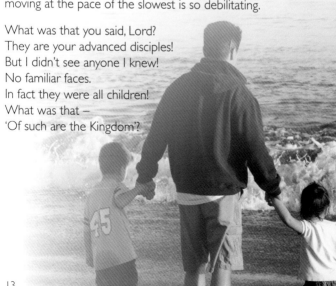

GOING HOME?

Going home?
He smiled –
I wish!
but I've a shift to finish.

Going home?
I'd need to say, sorry,
I'd never be accepted.
There's no room for me.
I've burnt my bridges,
too much has been said,
too little done to mend the hurt.

Mention home –
my stomach turns;
I feel crowded,
smothered,
afraid.

Which home?
My mother's home?
My father's home?
I've had many homes.
The question unsettles me,
makes me sad.
It reminds me of something
I've lost but never had.
Faith.

LIVING IN TIME AND ETERNITY

Oh God,
you have created us to live in time,
yet you have set eternity in our hearts.
Such a strange contradiction
we are,
are we not?
In time we believe,
in eternity we doubt,
yet in time we die
while in eternity we long to live:
such contradictions.
Cause us to ponder
our futility of thought;
no words,
no sounds,
no colours,
no shapes
can adequately
describe our longing
to know,
to be known
and embraced by you.

Thank you for
the morning bird song,
so pure and natural,
for the sky ablaze
with the glow of a setting sun,
for a word of hope
spoken by a prophet,
for the word of life
living as Jesus.
Oh God,
you have created me to live in time
so I might meet the contradiction of mystery
and be affirmed through faith.

THE MYSTERY OF DEATH

Oh Lord,
I don't like thinking this way.
In the morning I'm always so negative.
I want to live more,
give more,
I've so much still to do;
there's so much beauty all around
crying out to be explored:
a smile,
a book,
a poem,
a song,
a dance;
but each day
I die a little.
Do you really know the date of my death?
Dying itself is such a mystery,
it sounds so final,
but with you it's temporary.
The preacher said
it wasn't your resurrection that was a miracle,
it was the fact that you died.
Resurrection was the easy part for you,
for you dying was the impossible idea.
I can hear hell shouting – "God is dead",
yet nothing is impossible with you.

Lord,
help me to learn from the mystery of your death;
it's all part of the cycle of creation;
a seed dies only to produce a crop.
Help me live well today,
to work hard,
to die to self and live for you.

ETERNITY ON THE TANNOY

To be standing in the midst of chaos,
like a traveller passing through the night;
to feel there'll be no tomorrow
if you don't get on the next flight.
An announcement on the tannoy
tries to reassure your mind,
but the voice is so familiar
you could be listening to yourself;
to be walking in the midst of protest
like a prophet full of doubt,
to know there will be a judgement
even if the jury's out.

Then you read a headline in the newspaper
of what you dreamt the night before,
and it sounded so familiar,
like the opening of a door.
To be stumbling on the edge of freedom,
like a blind man gaining sight;
to take one step forward
and begin dancing in the light;
and a voice like a thousand rivers
roars a welcome not yet heard,
and eternity spins in silence,
leaving time to close the door.

WE'RE ALL DEAD MEN WALKING

Walking right off the planet,
pretending we're going nowhere
but knowing we're going somewhere.
Like feet on a moving airport escalator
we walk,
we don't walk –
makes no difference.
We're still moving,
we can't stop;
we're moving towards the gate;
we'll soon fly away.

We're all dead men walking:
looking for resurrection,
longing
to breathe again,
to smile again,
to love again,
to cry again,
to be again;
but dead men can't walk backwards.

We're all dead men walking –
living as we die,
dying as we live,
listening to voices
whispering in the background.
In the static,
voices from the past.
You're nothing;
you're as the wind,
yet straining to hear
the one voice above the many,
shouting:
you've got a future,
you're alive in Christ,
you've been born again.
You're living to walk into eternity.

THINKING THROUGH A SCREEN

Oh God,
here I am
praying,
thinking about you through a screen;
it's convenient,
but am I being truthful?
My computer system has just opened up:
I often think what would happen
if I opened up,
spoke to you like a friend,
asked you what you think of me;
but I won't ask
because I don't understand myself.
I actually don't understand how this all works.
Computers, faith and me are incompatible;
but I use it — because it delivers.
The whole box is a mystery.
I guess I live in the midst of mystery;
I'm a mystery myself;
I don't really know what I'm capable of.
I can love and hate all at the same time;
I can lie and cheat
and still think I'm as good as the next guy —
better than a computer!
I think that's the mystery.

Lord,
I'm sorry I trust my computer
more than you.
Help me to open up my life,
run your programme,
trust the mystery of so-called grace,
open my eyes,
open my ears,
and open my hands
to touch your mystery today.

THE DEFINITIVE G-MAIL

Oh Lord,
I'm back in the same place again.
My eyes are not quite open yet.
Sleep is an amazing gift,
and you invented it.
It's a mystery –
I mean, where do we go
when we sleep?
Time seems to be suspended;
we dream dreams;
do you speak to us through dreams?
I wish I could go to sleep right now;
soon I'll be scrolling through emails,
making up replies,
deleting the spam,
waiting for answers.

Lord,
I often wait for answers from you;
I get an awful lot of heavenly spam;
you know what I mean:
people who mean well,
giving advice.
I wait for the big one,
the definitive g-mail.
How long must I wait
to know your thoughts,
to win your approval,
to receive the call?

"When God is silent he is still speaking" –
why did that thought come into my head?
Maybe I need to understand silence,
listen to silence,
just be silent,
maybe more silent today.

WHAT DO YOU THINK ABOUT POLITICS ?

Excuse me, Lord,
but with all this politicking going on at Westminster,
someone asked me, what way would you vote?
Got me thinking.
Do you expect your disciples
to get involved with politics?
Mind you, the first lot were involved!
Judas was a right zealot.
He wanted you to declare UDI.
The apostles were a mixed bag.
The brothers James and John,
they believed
you could have taken over the government.
They wanted to be your right hand men
when you took power.
I think they must have misread the signs.
They thought you were literally standing for office.
Now Judas -
was he really all about freedom fighting?
You know I think you nailed it down when you said,
"Render to Caesar what is Caesar's
and to God what is God's".

Lord,
help me to make those distinctions more clearly.
Give me the courage to stand up for the things
I know to be true and just.
If I have to protest, help me do it because it is right.
Lord, help me to understand the power I have
when I clasp two hands together and say – 'Father…'
The more I pray,
the more I protest,
not simply with words
but with my life.

Lord,
help me pray a life.
Now is that not
pretty radical,
and even political?

JESUS, ARE YOU A CHARISMATIC OR A PRESBYTERIAN?

Lord,
I was just wondering -
which church would you attend?
Would you still want to go to the Synagogue?
Would you be a Presbyterian?
A Roman Catholic?
A Baptist perhaps?
Maybe you'd be a Charismatic?
I mean, after all,
you are really into healing and miracles!
Lord, I am asking this because
I'm not sure you'd fit into our church.
We like things to be predictable,
respectable and dignified.
We're serious,
but not too serious.
You may be just a bit too radical for our culture.
You see, we might "think it"
but you "say it".
I don't think the Vacancy Committee
would choose you.
You don't mind me being honest?
You know – speaking my mind?
Lord,
you really gave the Scribes a hard time.
Not to mention the Pharisees.
You didn't take prisoners.
You were about people over precedent.
What would you think of all our red tape? –
our Kirk Session,
our church laws,
our services,
our robes,
our pews,
our way of doing things?
Lord, you said,
you'd love it – if it's from the heart?
Ah, now you've got me!

STICKS AND STONES

Sticks and stones and broken bones
and terrorists and mobile phones
and babies cry alone;
children play and mothers pray
their children will be suicide bombers.
It's a strange world.
We live in desperate times.
The lines of right and wrong
have all been redrawn,
and suicide means — taking sides.
For some it's just another day
to hide, to pretend,
to say, "It's gonna be alright",
knowing nothing's right
and never will be till the guns stop
and soldiers go home
and poppies fall in Albert Hall,
and all around is silent;
no-one speaks a word.

Walking back home:
sore feet,
sore head,
sore heart,
so tired,
so sorry,
so what.

Walking back home:
still seeking, still weeping,
still reaping; say something,
say nothing, say everything.
Walking back home:
no promises, no compromises,
November;
too slow to know,
to say nothing;
instead, I'm forgiven;
words fail me.

NOVEMBER SUNDAY MORNING

Cold damp November Sunday morning:
boots and berries, top and toe,
comrades who once fought a common foe.
They march in solidarity to remember
what they have tried to forget.
It's sixty five years for some
since the guns fell silent.
For others the guns still pound
in their heads and in their hands,
Their wounds are still fresh.
Flesh and blood bind them together
like brothers and sisters in each other's arms.
They love, they fight,
they give themselves to each other
to protect the other.
Actions speak louder than guns.
In the face of struggle they act as one,
no-one turns back.
All have placed their life on the line.

Cold damp November Sunday morning.
Bodies lie limp and useless
under a warm downie;
they sleep,
they rest,
they dream.
They can't forget;
they won't remember;
they've closed their eyes,
and in their sleep they become the silent major-
ity
who stand for nothing and fall for anything,
who turn their head and ignore
the plight of a Mandela, or a Suu Kyi,
or a soldier in the crossfire.

Cold damp November Sunday.
Just two minutes –
too busy,
too late to Remember.

CROSSED OUT

Lord,
I like to see all the 'i's dotted and the 't's crossed?
I don't like mess;
I like everything in its right place.
I actually like to be in control.
I like to know what's going to happen.
I like to be prepared for every circumstance.

Lord,
I can't think what the world would be like
without my input, my experience, my perspective.
I know I sound self-centred but I know you'll understand –
it's just the way I'm made.

Lord,
I couldn't possibly cross over.
I like to dot my 'i's –
I could never cross an 'i'.
It would change from a letter
to a symbol
to a word.
I'd lose control;
I'd be crucifying myself.

Lord,
what if I changed my dot to a line? –
crossed myself out,
changed my 'i' to a 't'-shaped cross;
prayed, "Not my will but yours",
picked up the cross and followed.
Where would it lead me?
I'd end up looking foolish,
struggling, suffering,
perhaps deserting the cause.
My suffering couldn't add to my redemption.
You did it all, I can add nothing.

"My child: your 't'-shaped cross
could never spell redemption;
't' is the first response –
the first letter of a thankful heart."

ANGELS TALKING REVOLUTION

Yahweh,
I read with interest the story of Zachariah,
a priest,
struggling to talk
in your presence
while angels talk of revolution.
They talk of changing the regime.
It's not quite the Christmas story
as I have come to know it –
or maybe it is?
Maybe it's the Christmas story
I've refused to see
and others live each day:
turmoil,
trouble,
fear.
Lord,
were you not a refugee on the run?
Nothing changes.
The world is still looking for a Saviour –
a leader,
perhaps even a Messiah.
Yahweh,
forgive us when we are too blind to see.

MUMBLING PRAISE

Oh God,
how you have surprised me.
I thought everything was lost.
I was standing in your presence,
pretending,
mumbling words,
my lips out of sync with my thoughts,
my voice out of tune with my heart.
Ministry and disappointment
too often go together.
I'm the expert;
I've learned to perform under strain,
to do my job,
but I've always felt insecure;
I knew that you knew all about me.
Then you surprise me,
you give me the news,
you let me in on heaven's secret.

Yahweh —
you never forget,
you remembered your people;
even hypocrites can be redeemed.

Yahweh —
look, I'm not mumbling anymore.
You saved me from myself!

KEEP MY FEET ON THE GROUND

Yahweh,
I'm full of so much joy,
I'm grinning like a Cheshire cat.
You remembered your promises to me.
Help me not to forget the bad days;
help me to remember
while I'm singing
another is crying.
Heaven may have broken through for me,
but for others
there are no angels,
only long-standing promises that look empty.
Help me remember
the feeling of waiting for change,
the struggle of believing against the odds.

Yahweh,
I'm in a good place now.
Save me from being proud,
protect me from feeling smug.

Yahweh,
keep my feet on the ground
even if I talk with an angel.

FOLLOW ME!

Follow me! (You said).
How I wish you did call me to follow.
Just to be going somewhere,
to be leaving,
to be getting ready,
to be packing a suitcase,
to be packing a bag.
The only packing I do is at Tesco.
(God, I hate shopping!)
I need to move on;
change my life,
change my job,
change the way I think!
Moving means leaving;
leaving means making choices.
What do I take with me?
What do I leave behind?
I've so much "stuff" –
the kind of stuff that clings to you,
weighs you down,
makes you who you are.
It's stuff you can't leave behind.
What would I do with 'me'
if I left it all behind?
It's not just things,
it's people, ideas, beliefs,
attitudes, relationships.
Just say I was to go,
get up,
leave everything – beliefs, theology,
all that I struggle with in life
in religion, in politics.
What would I need to take with me?
What is it that I can't really leave behind?

The Word of Life,
a map for living;
the Bread of Life,
food for the soul;
the Wine of Life,
renewing my spirit;
the Water of life,
refreshing the mind,

SOWER GOD

Sower God, you sow seeds on our path,
on our journey, on our lives,
dreams, hopes, ambitions.
Everything you sow is good.
Help us guard the good, keep out the doubt.
We will not allow the darkness to steal our light.

Sower God,
you never give up sowing the seed.
Forgive us when we promise so much
and deliver so little.
When we stand so tall one day
and wither in the heat of the next day.
Make us fertile soil for your word;
guard our hearts, give us staying power;
help us to follow without counting the cost.

Sower God,
remove the spirit of uncertainty from our souls;
reap a harvest in our lives;
let the fruit of your Spirit grow up,
harvest peace, harvest joy, harvest love;
help us "Guard the Harvest",
grow in grace and share the fruit.

Sower God,
set up godly scarecrows in our lives;
chase evil from our door.
Open our heart to your seed;
in the stillness of the darkness
stir up the gift of faith;
break open the seed into life.
We will guard the good and feed the seed.

Sower God,
break up the rough ground in us;
plant your seed deep in our hearts;
take root and grow.
We will guard the good and feed the seed.

Sower God,
water the seed and cause your face to shine on us;
let your word grow up tall in our lives
as we reach to touch the Son.
We will guard the good and feed the seed.

THERE IS A RIVER

I think this river is
laughing with me.
It too has a place in the city.
God has given rivers a future;
now I know why it's singing in tune with the stones and
the fish.
Its presence lifts your spirit.
It really knows how to move;
it never stays still.
A river is always going somewhere,
flowing,
faster,
slower,
deeper,
broader.
I want to move with the river;
I want to race the river;
I want to swim in the water;
I want to catch a fish in the river;
I want to flow like the river.
Lord, let the river of life flow through me:
today,
yesterday,
and forever.

I NEED TO LEARN ABOUT RESTING

Lord,
today is your day.
I know every day is yours,
but today is a special day.
You made it different,
you made it holy,
you made it for rest and recreation,
and you called it Sabbath.
Help me to enjoy every moment of it.
Help me walk just a little slower,
talk just a little kinder,
listen just a little longer;
and, when I want to hurry things along,
remind me
most things will keep;
for you are the keeper of all our souls.

Lord,
teach me how to rest in your presence,
still my restless heart,
change this day from a day of trading
to a day of praising,
from a day of shopping
to a day of praying.
Lord,
I want to honour you today.

Chill Out

Dear Lord,
this is Sunday.
Help me keep it special,
different from all the rest.
Slow me down today,
let me feel Your presence
as I move through each hour.
I want to walk at Your pace,
discover Your path
and walk in it.

Lord,
I'm listening for Your word
I'm looking for the signs.
Draw near to me,
reassure my restless heart,
let me receive Your peace today.

ISBN 978-0-95667

9 780956 6